About this book

How many of us know about other religions of the world?
Do we ever wonder why some of our friends have different
beliefs from our own? There are today about 500 million
Buddhists in the world. How do they live and what are the
teachings that they follow? In this book Martha Patrick
traces the development of Buddhism and tells how it has
spread over the last 2500 years.

The book is illustrated with forty-nine photographs and
there is a glossary, a further reading list, and an index.

Buddhists and Buddhism

Martha Patrick

Wayland

Other books in this series

Christians and Christianity
Hindus and Hinduism
Jews and Judaism
Moslems and Islam
Sikhs and Sikhism

First published in 1982 by
Wayland (Publishers) Limited
49 Lansdowne Place, Hove
East Sussex BN3 1HF, England

2nd impression 1984

ISBN 0 85340 906 4

Printed and bound in Great Britain by
R. J. Acford, Industrial Estate, Chichester, Sussex.

Contents

1 Buddhism and Buddhists

Buddhism is one of the great religions of the world. For over 2,500 years people have found that the teachings of the Buddha are full of wisdom and kindness to others. Today over 500 million people living all over the world are Buddhist. What exactly do Buddhists believe in? Where did this religion begin? Who was the Buddha?

Buddhists follow the teachings of 'Buddha' or 'Enlightened One'. This was the title given to an Indian prince called Sidhatta Gotama who lived six hundred years before Christ. Sidhatta was not a god – he was a teacher who never claimed to be anything other than a human being. His father was the ruler of a kingdom in north India. For a time the young prince lived in his palace with a beautiful wife and son and every luxury he wanted. Sidhatta's father tried to keep all knowledge of worldly sorrows from his son's eyes. One day though, the young prince went out from the palace in a chariot and saw first an old man, then a sick man, then a dead man. At the sight of each he asked his charioteer the meaning of what he saw. 'This comes to all men,' said the charioteer. The prince also saw a wandering monk. Sidhatta returned to the palace troubled by what he had seen. He began to question why people should suffer and become sick and die. He felt a call to find out the meaning of life and so he said goodbye to his sleeping wife and child and left the palace.

Later he cut off his hair and exchanged his princely robes with those of a beggar and 'went forth into the homeless life'. For six years he wandered about the valley of the Ganges, meeting famous religious teachers. He studied with

Buddha Gaya in North India where the Buddha attained enlightenment.

7

Above *A temple carving showing the Buddha's first sermon.*

Below *The Ganges valley in the land of the Buddha.*

At Buddha Gaya there is a tree like the one under which the Buddha sat.

them but he was still not satisfied and had not found the answer to his questions, so he tried his own way. It was one evening, seated under a tree, that Sidhatta found the answer, – he became 'enlightened'. Afterwards Sidhatta became known as 'the Buddha', meaning 'the Enlightened one'. Enlightenment is sometimes called 'Nirvana'. It is the spiritual goal of every Buddhist.

After his 'Enlightenment' the Buddha decided that he wanted to help other people reach their own Enlightenment, so he began to teach. Very soon the Buddha attracted many followers and disciples who wanted to try out his teachings in their lives. In this way Buddhism began in the north of India 2500 years ago.

9

2 What did the Buddha teach?

The Buddha said that in life there is much suffering. This is understood by Buddhists to include all the problems of the world and personal ones too, both in the body and mind. Although the Buddha said that life is full of suffering, he was not gloomy because he also taught a way to find peace, happiness and enlightenment. The way the Buddha taught was to live by the 'Four Noble Truths'.

The Four Noble Truths are:

Suffering is a part of life.
Suffering is due to selfishness.
Suffering will stop if selfishness is overcome.
The way to bring suffering to an end is to follow the Eightfold Path.

Opposite *A Buddhist monastery in the Himalayas near Mount Everest.*

Left *Inside a Buddhist temple in Burma.*

The Eightfold Path is:

Accept the Four Noble Truths.
Think in the right way which leads you to help others.
Be kind in speech, avoid boasting, gossip and lies.
Do what is right.
Earn your living in a way which is good.
Avoid evil thoughts and actions and work hard.
Learn to meditate.
Be at peace in your mind.

Buddhist teachings were written down on pillars by the order of the Buddhist Emperor Asoka who lived in the third century BC.

Once the Buddha spoke to his followers of three fires: the feelings of greed, hatred and laziness. Sometimes these feelings may be so strong that they feel like a fire burning inside. A Buddhist tries to bring these fires under control by following the Eightfold Path. The Buddha spoke about many subjects, but the Four Noble Truths and the Eightfold Path are to be found at the centre of all he taught.

3 The growth of Buddhism

In India at the time of the Buddha, the existing religion was Brahmanism. This religion later developed into what is today known as Hinduism. In Brahmanism and Hinduism there are many complicated beliefs and ceremonies including the worship of deities. But the Buddha did not consider these important. Instead the Buddha in his own life pointed to a way, which, he said, would ease the suffering of man and bring happiness and peace to all.

Three hundred years after the Buddha's death a great Indian emperor became a Buddhist. His name was Asoka. He

*Inside a Zen monastery
in Japan.*

showed that it was possible to apply the Buddha's teachings of non-violence, peace and love. For many centuries in India, Buddhism existed alongside Hinduism until 1100 AD when the religions of Islam and Hinduism spread through and dominated the country. Today there are once again Buddhists in India, although the majority of Indians are Hindus.

Several hundred years after the Buddha's death, the Buddha's followers, who were monks, began to disagree about what the Buddha had taught. One group called the Thervada said that the real teaching of the Buddha was to be found in his sermons. The other group called the Mahayana developed the Buddha's teachings to include a great many other ideas. The monks held several Councils for discussion, but could not reach an agreement. Although different, many of the teachings of the two Schools are complementary and equally important. For example the Theravadins think the gaining of wisdom is important, while the Mahayanists think kindness to others is more important than acquiring knowledge. At an early date, Theravada Buddhism spread southwards from India. Emperor Asoka sent ambassadors to Ceylon, now called Sri Lanka, and others went to Burma. Thailand also became a Theravada Buddhist country.

Mahayana Buddhism was introduced to China around the first century AD. There already existed in China the two philosophies of Confucianism and Taoism. Buddhism was at first considered unimportant. It was partly the work of the monk Boddhidharma in the sixth century AD that made Buddhism more acceptable to the Chinese. He founded a School of Chinese Buddhism which soon became very popular. Boddhidharma's teaching later spread to Japan where it is known as Zen Buddhism. Today Buddhism has declined in China, and Confucianism is more popular.

Buddhism came to Japan in the sixth century AD. The Mahayana school was soon split into several Japanese schools who followed different beliefs. Today two of the main schools in Japan are the Pure Land Teaching and Zen.

Outside a Buddhist temple in Japan.

The Pure Land Teaching school has a character of its own and differs from the original Buddhist teachings. Pure Land Buddhists, more often known as Shin Buddhists, worship Amida whom they believe is the Buddha reborn as kindness and love. They hope for salvation after death in a Pure Land.

Zen Buddhism was founded by Boddhidharma in the sixth century AD. He said there should be 'No dependence upon words and letters'. Instead the most important task was to see into one's own nature. Today Zen Buddhism has many followers in Europe and America. The popularity of Zen is partly due to the way Zen places importance on practice rather than ideas and knowledge gained from books. The practice, as an old Zen poem says:

'The Perfect Way is without difficulty,
Save that it avoids picking and choosing.
Only when you stop liking and disliking
Will all be clearly understood.'

The goal of Zen Buddhists is 'Satori' or Enlightenment. Satori may be a sudden realization, but it is impossible to put the experience into words.

Buddhism was introduced into Tibet during the seventh century. Primitive beliefs in nature, gods and magic combined with other influences to develop a unique school of Buddhism. Tibetan Buddhism includes a great range of activities from mysterious, symbolic ceremonies to the worship of deities. The deities are names and human-like forms given to forces of nature. For example the 'Bodhisattva Avalokiteshvara' is compassion or loving kindness.

Right *A painting of Boddhidarma. It is said that he had a fierce gaze and that he was strict in his teaching.*

Left *The Dalai Lama with members of the Tibetan community who now live in England.*

Today Tibet is governed by China and the practice of Buddhism has been restricted. The religious and political leader of the Tibetans is the Dalai Lama. The Tibetans consider him to be a living form of Avalokiteshvara and a 'Buddha' or 'Enlightened person'. He now lives in exile in India.

Although there are many mysterious beliefs in Tibetan Buddhism, it does also include pure Buddhist teachings. Today in Europe and America, Tibetan Buddhism has many followers and there are many lamas living and teaching in the West. The title 'Lama' means 'superior one', and usually they are monks. The relationship of teacher to pupil in Buddhism is a very important one.

A Burmese father teaching his son how to light a candle as an offering to the Buddha.

4 Buddhists – the people

There is no special ceremony or 'baptism' to become a Buddhist. If a person thinks the Buddha's teaching is right, he follows the Eightfold Path in his own life and then he is a Buddhist. The Buddhist way of life is simply in all you do not to harm other living beings and to help others as much as possible. Their wish not to harm other beings means that many Buddhists are vegetarians and would not fight in a war, though this is not a rule.

'Think in the right way which leads you to help others' is part of the Eightfold Path. In a Buddhist family the child thinks of his parents as almost holy. The child knows that he has to look after his parents in their old age, to work for the good name of the family, and to look after the money

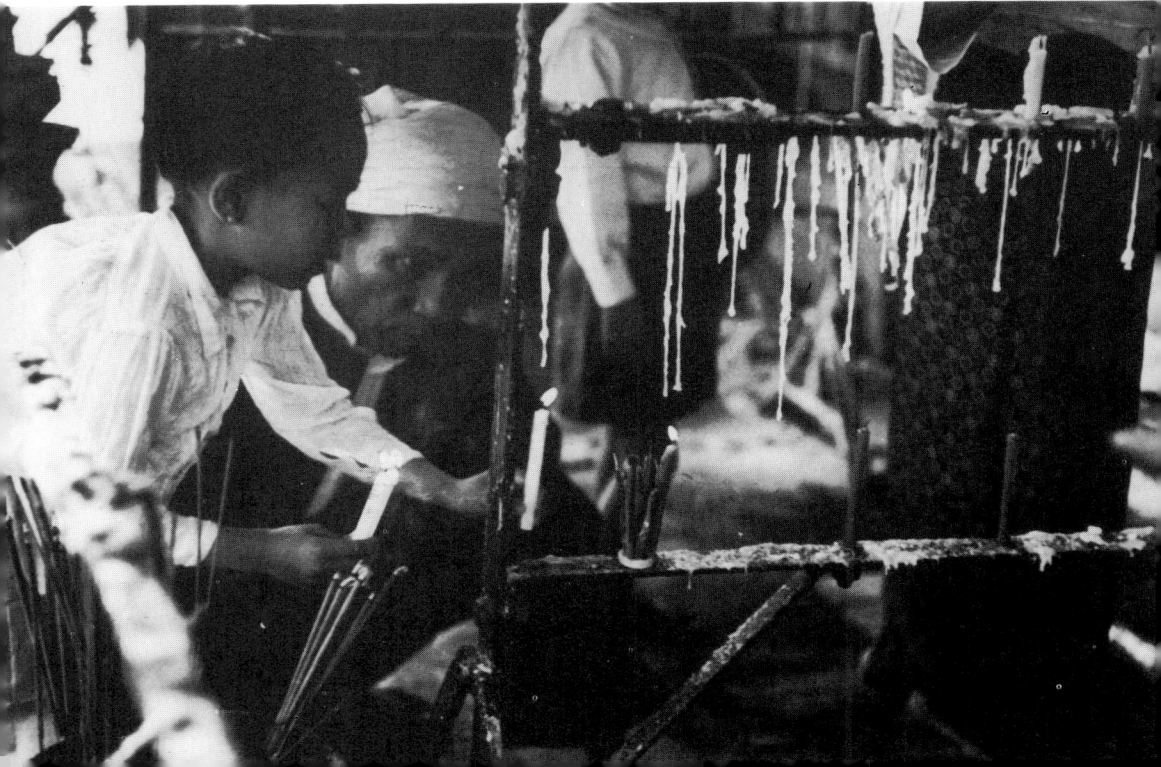

belonging to it. Buddhist parents try to keep their children from bad influences and they try to give their children a good education. They also help to arrange the marriage of their children into good families. Parents try to leave their children property when they die.

In Buddhist countries there are large numbers of monks. There are monasteries near many towns. As well as looking after his own family, a Buddhist feels he has a special duty to give food and money to the monks.

Another part of the Eightfold Path is 'avoid evil thoughts and work hard'. Many Buddhists understand this as to avoid being tempted to become lazy, greedy or angry. As animals are trained so Buddhists try to train themselves. Many Buddhists learn verses like these by heart:

As the elephant endures the arrow, so will I patiently bear abuse, for many in the world are unkind.
The trained elephant is mounted by the King and led in

A Buddhist temple in
Tibet.

procession. The self-controlled man who bears abuse
patiently is the best among men.
Mules and horses and elephants are excellent when
trained, but more excellent is the man who has trained
himself.
A man does not reach Enlightenment mounted on any
animal, but by training himself.

The orchestra of a temple
in Tibet, with the strange
instruments used to play
the religious music.

21

5 Statues of the Buddha

In Buddhist countries there are many statues of the Buddha. You can see the statues in people's homes and outside and inside temples. Buddhists bow before the statues and 'Go for Refuge' in the 'Triple Gem'. To 'Go for Refuge' means to find encouragement and happiness from following the Buddha — it is a dedication to the Buddha whom Buddhists believe showed a way to end suffering. The 'Triple Gem' is made up of 'the Buddha', his teaching which is called the 'Dharma', and other Buddhists all over the world who are called the 'Sangha'. Sometimes the Sangha means particularly the monks.

Bowing shows respect for something — by bowing down a person shows that he is not proud and that he knows that there are more important things in life than himself.

In their homes and temples, Buddhists place flowers in front of statues of the Buddha. They also light candles and lamps and burn incense. The Buddha said that all things in life are changing — flowers remind people of this. A flower grows, it blooms, then it dies away and somewhere else a new flower is coming into bud. The candles and lamps burning brightly are thought to be like the Buddha's teaching which shines with love and wisdom. The incense releases a fragrance into the air which is also thought to be like the Buddha's teaching.

To make offerings in front of shrines and statues of the Buddha is a way for people to show their respect for the Buddha's teachings. By making offerings people also show their dedication to the Eightfold Path. What a Buddhist does and how he treats other people is, however, more important

Inside a Buddhist temple in Japan.

A Chinese statue of the Bodhisattva Kuan Yin who represents peace and mercy.

than making offerings. Verses from one of the scriptures describe how 'The scent of flowers, incense and jasmine cannot travel against the wind, but the fragrance of good deeds travels in all directions. Sweeter than the scent of incense and jasmine is the perfume of good deeds.'

Elephants and their trainers in Sri Lanka, which is a Buddhist country.

6 Ceremonies and festivals

Ceremonies and festivals are held on special days to celebrate events in the life of the Buddha. In countries of the East these days are often a holiday from work for everyone. During ceremonies in the temples verses from Buddhist scriptures are chanted. In particular the Buddha is praised and then people 'Go for Refuge' in the 'Triple Gem' by saying three times, 'I go to the Buddha for Refuge, I go to the Dharma for Refuge, I go to the Sangha for Refuge.' Everyone will then say five rules of action they intend to live by. These are called 'Pansil' and are:

1. Not to harm or destroy life.
2. Not to steal.

Left *Many statues of the Buddha seen inside a Burmese temple.*

Right *A standing statue of the Buddha in Sri Lanka.*

3. Not to misuse sex or to commit adultery.
4. Not to tell lies.
5. Not to take intoxicating drinks which harm the mind and make you lazy.

Buddhists in the congregation usually recite these words, following the lead of a Buddhist monk. The people may also listen to a sermon given by a monk. At night there are often great candle-lit processions outside and round the inside of the temples. Dancing, music-making and feasting often take place too.

Buddhist festivals are held at the time of the full moon. An important one is in the lunar month around April and May. It is the Festival of the Full Moon called 'Wesak'. This festival celebrates the Buddha's birth, his Enlightenment

*Offering flowers in front
of a statue of the Buddha.*

and his death. Wesak is the Buddhist New Year.

Buddhist birth, marriage and death ceremonies vary from country to country and from school to school of Buddhism. In many places monks will participate in some way. They may chant from the scriptures or give a blessing or a sermon. The ceremonies often take place in a Buddhist monastery or temple.

A Buddhist procession.

7 Buddhist monks

After his Enlightenment the Buddha had found truth and freedom from suffering, but he knew how much greed, hatred and ignorance there was in the world, so he decided to spend the rest of his life encouraging people by explanation and example to find their own Enlightenment. The Buddha had about sixty disciples to help him. He said to them, 'Go ye now monks, and wander for the gain of the many, for the happiness of the many, out of compassion for the world, for the good, for the gain of everyone.' The monks

A Lama wearing a bull mask as the Lord of Death in a Tibetan dance festival.

travelled all over the world and the religion of Buddhism spread to many countries.

Today there are thousands of Buddhist monks all over the world. There are also Buddhist nuns, although there are fewer nuns than monks. A person who becomes a monk or nun has decided they want to give all their time to activities and studies which are purely Buddhist. They usually live in a monastery. They encourage other people by explaining the Buddha's teaching and by the example they set in their own lives. In the East, monasteries are often schools. In Burma, Thailand and Kampuchea every boy spends part of his childhood in a monastery. The Buddha taught in the Four Noble Truths that being selfish and wanting things for yourself is a cause of suffering. Monks learn to want nothing for themselves. They live with only what they need, not what they want. Their needs are simple: food, clothing, medicine and shelter.

Buddhist monks carrying alms bowls.

A monk may enter a monastery in the first place for a trial period and if he decides that the life is right for him, he may commit himself more definitely by becoming ordained. When he is ordained he is given a new name and a robe. In some countries the monks wear orange robes, while in other countries they wear yellow or black robes. The monks are easily recognized by their robes. They also shave their heads

A Buddhist funeral service held in England.

Left *A monk putting on his robe.*

Right *A lesson for Buddhist monks in Thailand.*

and often go about barefoot. A monk may decide to 'disrobe' at any time. To disrobe means to cease to be a monk.

Monks have no family or money of their own. They are given all their food. In Buddhist countries you can see monks leaving their monasteries at dawn with their alms bowls. They go on what is called the 'alms round'. A great mixture of food may be put into their bowls! The monks take what is given in silence. Sometimes they do not thank the person who gives them the food because Buddhists believe that the person who gives gains more; in giving you gain happiness by being a generous person. Other monks when they are walking with their alms bowls say verses from Buddhist scriptures. When they have been given some food the monks take their bowls back to the monastery. They then share together what they have been given. Meal-times in a monastery are like a special ceremony. In many monasteries

there is only one meal a day before noon. The monks eat whatever they are given. They eat together but they talk as little as possible. They are careful not to eat greedily. They eat quietly, with their attention on their own food.

Monks may only eat at meal-times. This is one of several rules in a monastery. The rules are to help monks to live a pure Buddhist life. The rules which are called the 'Pansil'. are as follows:

1. Not to destroy or harm life.
2. Not to steal.
3. The rule of chastity which is not to have sexual relations or marry.
4. Not to tell lies.
5. Not to take intoxicating drinks.
6. Not to eat other than at meal-times.

7. Not to go to entertainments like shows, with dancing or music.
8. Not to wear perfumes or scents or wear ornaments and decoration.
9. Not to sleep on comfortable raised beds.
10. Not to accept or handle gold or silver.

The first five rules of the Pansil for monks are like the Pansil other Buddhists say. The last five rules are to help monks to train themselves more strictly. They train themselves particularly not to be greedy or selfish.

In the Buddhist scriptures some verses describe what a monk should be like. (A monk may also be called a bhikkhu.)

'First of all the bhikkhu must guard his senses, be calm

Right *A monk receiving food in his alms bowl.*

Left *Some of Burma's 100,000 monks are seen here washing at a well in a temple enclosure.*

and obey the right rules. Even as faded leaves drop from the tree so must greed and hatred fall from the bhikkhu. A bhikkhu who has confidence in the Law will attain Nirvana and the end of suffering. The bhikkhu who applies the Law of the Buddha enlightens the world, just as the moon passing from behind clouds.'

The monks lead a simple life. They are like other people in that they too have to do the necessary daily chores, such as cooking, cleaning and gardening. But unlike other people they do not have a home, possessions or entertainments. They therefore have more time for the activities which they think are important. These activities are the study of Buddhist scriptures, teaching and meditation.

8 The art of meditation

Meditation is part of the Eightfold Path. Monks spend several hours a day meditating. Sometimes they get up before dawn at around 4.00 a.m. to meditate. Many Buddhists who are not monks or nuns meditate in their own homes. Meditation helps people to let their minds become purer. This means that they are less troubled by worrying thoughts and feelings like greed, hatred and laziness. By meditation a person aims to grow more kind towards others. Their aim is also to become wise so that they may be enlightened like the Buddha. Meditation is not like prayer because Buddhists do not believe in a personal God that they can pray to. Meditation is to do with thinking and feeling. In one sermon the Buddha encouraged his followers to make their love for all living beings grow by thinking . . . 'May all living beings be happy and secure; may their minds be contented.' 'Let not one in anger or ill will wish any harm to another.' 'Let thoughts of love go to all living beings all over the world without exception.'

Buddhists believe that thoughts of good and love lead a person to do kind things for others. From good thoughts and deeds only good results can happen while from bad thoughts and deeds only bad results happen. Buddhists call this the natural law of 'Karma'. The Buddha pointed out how people who have evil thoughts and do evil things will always suffer afterwards for it. Take for example a man who hates someone and kills them. He will suffer because people will call him a murderer and they will not trust him. He will suffer because he will be sent to prison. He may also be unhappy because he regrets what he has done. The murderer

The meal time in a
Japanese monastery.   *37*

makes his family unhappy too.

Another type of meditation the Buddha taught is called 'Mindfulness'. The Buddha suggested that people should try just feeling their breathing going in and out and do nothing else. In order to keep alert and still while breathing the Buddha advised people to sit with a straight back and with crossed legs. It is in this position that many Buddhists sit when they meditate and how the Buddha is often represented in statues. When a person concentrates on his breathing and nothing else he finds that fewer selfish and disturbing thoughts come to him and his mind becomes calmer and clearer. Buddhists try to give their full attention to whatever they do. It is said that 'it is good to train the wandering mind. A mind under control brings great happiness.'

The Buddha studied himself and others like a scientist. He encouraged people to meditate upon what their bodies are

*A young monk studying
the Buddhist scriptures.*

made of including the bones, tissue and fluids. The Buddha
pointed out how all life is born, grows, decays and dies and
new life is born somewhere else.

The Buddha said that people should also observe their
feelings and how different feelings come and go. There are
those feelings, for instance, which are pleasant or painful,
kind or greedy, lazy or hardworking. The Buddha thought
that if people could understand that all things are changing
there would be less suffering. Buddhists believe that meditation helps them to understand life more clearly. One
of the verses from the Buddhist scriptures describes how by
meditating earnestly the wise realize Nirvana, the highest
happiness.

A monastery in Japan.

9 The spread of Buddhism in the West

How was Buddhism first made known to people in the West? Until the nineteenth century in the western countries of the world, Buddhism was misunderstood and thought of as an Indian religion worshipping a God called Buddha. It was during the nineteenth century that a small number of men and women in Europe became seriously interested in Buddhism. They learned to read and speak the languages of Buddhist countries. They travelled in the East and visited monasteries and temples where they talked with monks and began to read and translate Buddhist scriptures.

Buddhist scriptures are not contained in one book like the Bible. There are many books. One of the main collections of books is called the Pali Canon. The translators began the large task of translating the Pali Canon and other books into the languages of the West including German, French, Italian and English. For the first time, instead of hearing stories about a strange eastern god called Buddha, people in the West were able to read about what the Buddha taught. They realized that the Buddha was not a god, but a wise and kind man who became 'enlightened'. People saw that the teachings of the Buddha can be followed anywhere in the world. Buddhists do not think of themselves as separate from other people because of their religion, nationality, class or colour. In the West Buddhists have found that they can live happily alongside Christians and people of other faiths.

At the beginning of the twentieth century there were only a few Buddhists in England. One man called R. J. Jackson used to stand on a box in Regent's Park, in London, lecturing on Buddhism to anyone who wanted to listen to him!

A Buddhist monk meets a boy dressed as a punk in England.

Later he helped to open a bookshop in London to sell Buddhist books. By that time a couple of Englishmen had visited the East and become Buddhist monks. They returned to England and helped to explain the Buddha's teaching to others.

In 1908 a monk from Burma called Ananda Metteya arrived in England to head the first Buddhist mission to the West. He wrote books and taught Buddhism. Ananda Metteya was the first of many hundreds of monks from countries in the East who have come to England.

In 1981 an important event for Buddhists in England took place. It was the visit of His Holiness the Dalai Lama. He is a monk and is called His Holiness because many Buddhists consider him to be an enlightened man like the Buddha. He is the political and religious leader of the Tibetan people. When he is in India, where he lives in exile, he lives the simple life of a monk. When he came to England he stayed with the Archbishop of Canterbury at Lambeth Palace in

Left *The Buddha and his attendants. Statues like these are seen in many Buddhist homes.*

Right *The lotus flower and a duck. In Buddhist art the lotus flower is often represented as a symbol of purity and beauty.*

London. In a church in London he gave a sermon. People of many different faiths listened to him. He spoke of the important Buddhist teaching to show love and understanding to people who belong to other religions. At another meeting, all the Buddhist teachers and monks from all schools of Buddhism in England gathered to hear the Dalai Lama. He spoke of the differences between the schools of Buddhism (Zen, Theravada, Tibetan, etc) and how for people living in England the differences are less important than the basic teachings of the Buddha. The basic teachings include the Four Noble Truths and the Eightfold Path which are common to all schools of Buddhism. The Dalai Lama also spoke to people of the way the world is changing and of the great advances in science and technology. The Dalai Lama pointed out how important world peace has become, if the human race is to survive. The population of the world has

43

grown and nations need to help each other. The Dalai Lama said all religions are important because they teach us to be less selfish and to be kind to others. He said the basic practice of Buddhism is never to harm others and to help others as much as possible.

Among the people who listened to the Dalai Lama were many English people who have become Buddhists. Today all over England there are Buddhist centres and monasteries. It is difficult to estimate how many Buddhists there are in this country. The majority of people living in England are Christian. Some Christians are interested in Buddhism and some Buddhists think both Christ and the Buddha were wise teachers.

One man who has played an important part in making Buddhism known to thousands of people is Christmas Humphreys. In 1918, when Humphreys was seventeen years old, he became interested in Buddhism after reading a book about it. In 1924 he founded a new Buddhist Society in London. It is still one of the main centres of Buddhism in England and is now the oldest and one of the largest Buddhist organizations in Europe. Christmas Humphreys studied law and became a judge. He soon became known as a Buddhist judge and an author of books on Buddhism. His feeling for prisoners was one of sympathy. He used to tell prisoners that it was not the judge who was punishing them but they were punishing themselves by doing wrong.

Christmas Humphreys' books on Buddhism have been read by people all over the world. He has often repeated the words of the Buddha when he told people not to be persuaded to become Buddhist out of respect for a religion or because they had read a book or heard good arguments. Instead, the Buddha said, try to live by the Four Noble Truths and the Eightfold Path. Try out for yourself the Four Noble Truths and the Eightfold Path, see if they work and are true. If so you can accept them and be a Buddhist.

Meditation on a cold day in England.

10 Buddhist communities in Britain

By following the Eightfold Path anyone can be a Buddhist. It is not necessary to go and live in a monastery to be a Buddhist. A child at school shows a true understanding of Buddhism if he tries not to be selfish and is kind to people he does not like. The child has a truer understanding of Buddhism than a monk if all the monk is interested in is himself. The Buddha said it is up to each person how they follow the Eightfold Path. He said, 'You yourself must make the effort.' He could only point the way to freedom from suffering and enlightenment.

As each Buddhist makes his own effort to follow the Buddha's teaching some people find that they want to share their life with other Buddhists who have similar interests. Sharing with others means you can encourage each other.

One large group of Buddhists who live and work together are called the Friends of the Western Buddhist Order. This order was established in 1967, and is often shortened to 'the Friends'. They have established many communities where young Buddhists live together. They also have centres where people can go for meditation classes and to meet other Buddhists. The friends have centres all over Britain and also abroad. In London there is a centre which used to be a fire station. It now includes two rooms containing statues of the Buddha. These rooms are called the 'shrine rooms'. They are used for meditation and classes. Some people live at the centres. They are called Order Members.

Order Members have decided that by working for the Friends they want to live for 'The Three Jewels', that is, the Buddha, his teaching (the Dharma) and other Buddhists (the Sangha). The Order Members help to tell their visitors and friends about Buddhism. They also run 'retreats'.

Left *The Archbishop of Canterbury and the Dalai Lama.*

Right *His Holiness the Dalai Lama.*

A retreat is for people who want to spend several days away from their ordinary life. On a retreat people study Buddhism, meditate and talk together. Retreats are often enjoyed as a change and a chance to think more deeply about life. One man after a retreat said that what he remembered was an atmosphere of laughter, warmth and joy.

Part of the Eightfold Path is 'Earn your living in a way which is good'. This is also called Right Livelihood. Money which is earned by harming others or by dishonesty is not right livelihood. Obviously, for example, selling guns or poisons is wrong livelihood. The Friends and many other Buddhists have decided that right livelihood for them means that in work everyone should share responsibilities. They think there should be no one who earns more than others. A 'co-operative' aims to make earning money a friendly business. The Friends say this way of working helps others and helps each person to grow towards his own enlightenment.

47

The *Dalai Lama meeting Buddhists.*

In the work of their co-operatives the Friends are pleased to make contact with people who do not know about Buddhism. The co-operatives include food shops where they sell foods which are natural and good for health. They also have restaurants which serve vegetarian food. Their co-operatives include building services and printing workshops.

The 'Friends of the Western Buddhist Order' are led by an Englishman who became a monk and who is now called the 'Venerable Sangharakshita'. He spent twenty years in the East studying the main schools of Buddhism. When he returned to England he began the Friends as a new school.

In England there are many other Buddhists who prefer to follow the Buddha's teachings as they are taught by the older Schools of Buddhism. There are many monks from Buddhist countries of the East who are now living in England. They lead, for instance, Tibetan, Theravada and Zen Centres. A person who is interested in Buddhism has therefore many schools of Buddhism to choose from. It is thought important to choose the school of Buddhism that suits each person's interests best.

Left *Christmas Humphreys and some monks at a celebration of Wesak in England.*

48

11 Life in a Buddhist monastery

One of the Buddhist monasteries which has been established in England is at Chithurst on the Sussex Downs. There are eight monks and four nuns and seven men who intend to become monks. In 1978 the monks were given 108 acres of wooded land. The monks then bought an almost derelict house nearby. This has now been repaired and has become a monastery which is surrounded by beautiful countryside.

The monks at Chithurst are known as bhikkhus. They follow the 'Forest Tradition' from the Theravada School of Buddhism as it is practised in Thailand. The forest bhikkhus live in a way which is very similar to the way of life of the bhikkhus in the time of the Buddha. They have few needs. They live in a quiet place in a forest. They develop 'mindfulness' through meditation and lead a strict life governed by rules of behaviour. In Thailand, monasteries in towns and villages are often like schools where bhikkhus study scriptures and teach. At Chithurst Monastery as in the forest

monasteries of Thailand, meditation is practised in the peace and quiet of the country.

The men who have become bhikkhus at Chithurst are all from countries of the West. Some say that when they found out about the way that Theravada monks lived they felt certain it was the right thing for them to do. One of the nuns at Chithurst says that she felt in her heart that the life was for her. The Abbot of Chithurst Monastery is called the Venerable Sumedho. After many years of studying Buddhism in Thailand the Venerable Sumedho now has permission from senior monks in Thailand to 'ordain' monks in England. When a man has lived in a monastery for several years and it is agreed that he is ready to become a bhikkhu he is 'ordained'. At a special ceremony he dedicates himself to the life of a bhikkhu. At Chithurst Monastery the ceremony

Left *The Friends' whole foods shop.*

Right *Friends of The Western Buddhist Order in their shrine room in London.*

takes place on a particular area of ground called the 'Sima'.

The bhikkhus at Chithurst live by the Buddha's rules in which he said monks should depend on ordinary people for material support which is mainly food and money. People should only give if they wish to. In return the monks should be able to give people spiritual support which includes the teachings of the Buddha. In this way Buddhist monks have contact with ordinary people. The bhikkhus at Chithurst are supported entirely by their friends and visitors. The Bhikkhus also continue the tradition of the 'alms round'. Every day they walk into the village nearby where they may receive gifts in their bowls. At first the sight of Buddhist monks in the English countryside surprised local people, but now they are more familiar with the bhikkhus in their orange robes!

The bhikkhus have 227 rules of behaviour to follow. The rules are written down in the Buddhist scriptures. The bhikkhus do not think there are too many rules or that it is too strict a discipline, instead they say the rules help them to become free from selfish desires. They learn to live with the barest necessity of food and sleep. They eat only one meal a day and they sleep from 10.00 p.m. until 4.00 a.m. when they get up to meditate. They also only talk when it is necessary. Another rule is that they are allowed no entertainments. If a bhikkhu finds that he wants some amusement or distraction for himself he reacts by just being 'mindful' of the desire and in this way he watches the desire come and go.

The bhikkhus and nuns are always fully occupied. Among the jobs at Chithurst monastery the nuns have cooking and cleaning and work in the garden to do. The bhikkhus have work in the forest and on their buildings. The monks strictly observe the rule not to harm living things. This means that they are not allowed to cut down trees in the forest. The bhikkhus, however, spend most of their time meditating, teaching and talking to visitors.

Some of the visitors to Chithurst monastery are families from Buddhist countries. They are used to giving food to monks and talking with them. Other English people visit the monastery to hear Buddhist teachings from the bhikkhus. The pure and simple way of life that the bhikkhus lead makes it possible for them to speak with a deeper understanding of the Buddha's teaching. At Chithurst, the bhikkhus and nuns are showing by their example that over 2,500 years after the Buddha's death his teachings can be closely followed in England.

12 The Jataka tales

The Buddhist scriptures consist of over 500 tales, adventure stories, fables, riddles, parables and comic tales which are said to have been told by the Buddha. The Buddha often used stories to show how his teachings work.

The Jataka tales are also called birth stories. In order to understand them we need to realize how Buddhists think of birth and death. After his Enlightenment the Buddha said, 'There is no more birth for me!' Before Enlightenment Buddhists observe that in life there is a continuous cycle of birth, growth, decay and death. Buddhists believe that a new life is the result of the actions in a past life. This is known as the law of 'Karma'. Buddhists do not share the Hindus' belief that an individual is reincarnated; instead Buddhists believe that life in all its forms is continually changing.

Left *The shrine room inside the monastery.*

*A Bhikkhu and Doris the
cat who live at Chithurst
monastery.*

According to the stories the Buddha was able to remember
his own and other people's previous lives. The story of the
misguided elephant was told by the Buddha when one of his
followers was brought to him and accused of following
another master. The other master was a wicked man who
claimed to be wise. The other master had gained the favour
of a king and lived in luxury eating perfumed three-year-old
rice with all the choicest flavouring. He cared only for his
own comfort and he had gained honour and respect by dishonesty. The Buddha said to his follower: 'How could you
follow the other master after you had heard my teachings –
can you not see that the other master is dishonest? Then
the Buddha said: 'I have noticed that you have always been

easily led astray and that you have followed in turn everyone you meet.' The Buddha then told this story of the past.

A king had an elephant called Damsel-face, who was virtuous and good and never hurt anybody. One night some burglars came and sat by the elephant's stall to discuss their plans. They agreed that it would not matter if they killed people for then there would be fewer people to resist them. They told each other they should get rid of all goodness and be men of cruelty and violence. For several nights the men came back and talked in this way. The elephant believed that the burglars had come to instruct him and that he too must become pitiless, cruel and violent. The next morning

The 'Sima'.

One of the nuns by the
nuns' cottage near the
monastery at Chithurst.

when his keeper appeared Damsel-face dashed him to death on the ground.

The news was brought to the King that Damsel-face had gone mad and was killing people, so the King sent for a wise man and said, 'Go, wise man, and see what has happened to Damsel-face.' The wise man went and soon saw that Damsel-face was not ill. The wise man then realized what the cause of the change must be. He asked the elephant keepers if any people had been talking near to the elephant's stall. The keepers said some burglars had been seen nearby. The wise man then returned to the King and told him there was nothing wrong with Damsel-face physically, but that he had been influenced and changed by overhearing some burglars talking. The King then said: 'Well, what is to be done now?' The wise man answered, 'Order good men to sit near the elephant and talk of goodness.' Good people went near the elephant and said, 'Do not mistreat or kill. The good should be patient, loving and merciful.'

After this story the Buddha said to his follower who had left him for another master: 'You were Damsel-face in those days and I was the wise man.'

13 Death of the Buddha

Just before the Buddha died he asked his disciples and followers if they had any questions or doubts about his teaching. No one answered him. He asked again and said, 'Do not be silent out of reverence because I am your teacher. Speak as a friend would to a friend.' Again there was no reply. The Buddha was then satisfied that all his followers were on their own Path to Enlightenment. His last words were, 'All living things will pass away. Try to accomplish your aim with steady effort.'

The Death of the Buddha.

Glossary

Bhikkhu The name for a Buddhist monk of the Theravada school.

Buddha The name meaning 'Enlightened One' which was given to Sidhatta Gotama 600 years BC.

Bodhisattva A person or deity who is dedicated to be kind and to help others.

Dalai Lama The political and religious leader of the Tibetans. He is thought to be an 'Enlightened person'.

Dharma The Buddha's teachings in the widest sense.

Eightfold Path The way the Buddha taught to bring an end to suffering.

Enlightenment The spiritual goal of every Buddhist. It is described as the 'Absolute Truth'. A state of peace and freedom from impurities like greed, hatred and ignorance.

Four Noble Truths A description of suffering as part of life, the cause of suffering and the way to end suffering.

Go for Refuge Dedication to the Buddha, the Dharma and the Sangha.

Karma The law that good actions have good results and bad actions have bad results. The results are experienced in this life or in a rebirth.

Lama A Buddhist monk of the Tibetan school.

Mahayana The Northern School of Buddhism found in Tibet, Mongolia, China, Korea and Japan. It has many forms and branches.

Meditation A special attention given to thoughts and actions. It is learning to train the mind.

Mindfulness Another type of meditation taught by the Buddha.

Nirvana The highest form of Enlightenment.

Pansil A vow to oneself to obey certain rules not to do wrong.

Pali Canon Books of the main and earliest Buddhist scriptures.

Rebirth The belief that a new life is the result of the actions of a past life.

Robe Garments worn by monks. The colour varies according to the country and school of Buddhism.

Sangha The brotherhood of firstly the Buddhist monks and secondly all other Buddhists.

Therevada The Southern School of Buddhism found in Sri Lanka, Burma and Thailand.

Triple Gem The Buddha, the Dharma, the Sangha.

Wesak A festival commemorating the Buddha's Birth, Enlightenment and Passing.

Damsel-face and the burglars.

More books

What the Buddha taught. Walpole Rahula (Gordon Fraser).

Introducing Buddhism. Irmgard Schloegl (Zen Centre, obtainable from Buddhist Society).

Buddhism. Christmas Humphreys (Pelican).

Dhammapada. (Buddhist Society or Penguin).

Selected Buddhist Scriptures. (Penguin).

Zen Mind, Beginner's Mind. S. Suzuki (obtainable from Buddhist Society).

The Life of the Buddha. H. Saddhatissa (Allen and Unwin).

A Short History of Buddhism. Edward Conze (Allen and Unwin).

Index